The Healing of a Wounded Heart

Prayerful Reflections on the Samaritan Woman Story

Laura Marie Durant

Nihil obstat: Reverend Henry Carter Finch, Censor
St. Peter Catholic Student Center, Waco, Texas

Imprimatur: +Joe S. Vásquez, S.T.L., D.D.
Bishop of Austin

The *nihil obstat* and the *imprimatur* are a declaration that a book is considered to be free of doctrinal or moral error. It is not implied that those who have granted the *nihil obstat* and the *imprimatur* agree with the concerns, opinions, or statements expressed therein.

The Healing of a Wounded Heart:
Prayerful Reflections on the Samaritan Woman Story

Copyright © 2022 by Laura Marie Durant

All rights reserved. No part of this publication may be reproduced, distributed, or transmitted in any form or by any means, including photocopying, recording, or other electronic or mechanical methods without the prior written permission of the publisher, except in the case of brief quotations embodied in critical reviews and certain other noncommercial uses permitted by copyright law.

Scripture texts in this work are taken from the *New American Bible, revised edition* © 2010, 1991, 1986, 1970 Confraternity of Christian Doctrine, Washington, D.C., and are used by permission of the copyright owner. All Rights Reserved. No part of the New American Bible may be reproduced in any form without permission in writing from the copyright owner.

ISBN 978-1-7330439-1-5

*To the women of St. Margaret Mary
Catholic Church in Cedar Park, Texas.*

*You are known by Him.
You are loved by Him.
You are cherished by Him.*

Contents

Introduction 1
How to Use This Book 3
Prayer One: *Jesus, take me to places unknown* 7
Prayer Two: *Jesus, thank You for lowering Yourself to our human state* 13
Prayer Three: *Jesus, thank You for always reaching out to me* 19
Prayer Four: *Jesus, enlighten my heart with the truths of heaven* 25
Prayer Five: *Jesus, quench my thirst with the ocean of mercy in Your Heart* 31
Prayer Six: *Jesus, cleanse me from my sins and restore my heart anew* 37
Prayer Seven: *Jesus, help me to praise You with my whole heart.* 43

Prayer Eight: *Jesus, set my heart on fire with the truth of who You are* 49

Prayer Nine: *Jesus, be with me in my lack of understanding* 55

Prayer Ten: *Jesus, I want to love like You* 61

Prayer Eleven: *Jesus, help me to live on the bread of life alone* 67

Prayer Twelve: *Jesus, help me to sow the seeds of Your love* 73

Prayer Thirteen: *Jesus, may You reign in my heart for all eternity* 79

About the Author 85

Introduction

Who doesn't need a heart transformation?

We've all be wounded, and we've all sinned because of our wounds. At some point, we've all felt rejection, betrayal, and shame. And no doubt, these wounds can lead to isolation, depression, anxiety, and despair. They can also spawn sins, such as jealousy, envy, and the deadliest one of all, pride.

But there is hope and healing in the Heart of Jesus. There is mercy beyond our greatest imagination.

When I began my own healing journey, by the mercy of God, I was drawn to healing accounts in Scripture. For me, there is no more compelling journey of healing and transformation than the story of the Samaritan woman.

I easily related to her story. Like many others, I know all too well the pain of rejection, the sting of betrayal, and the consuming burden of shame. I also know how easy it is to seek out love in the wrong places and the wrong ways to soothe the aching pain of feeling unwanted, unworthy, and unlovable. And, most unfortunately, I know the destruction of sin.

Fortunately, for the Samaritan woman and myself (and you!), Jesus came to save, not to condemn.

The prayerful reflections on the Samaritan woman story shared in this book reveal how Jesus transformed a wounded heart. It is the Samaritan woman's story, but it is also mine. Could it be yours?

I invite you to take this prayerful journey with the Samaritan woman as she engages with Jesus. See how gentle He is with her heart and how He tends to her every need as she moves through the healing process.

It is in the Most Sacred Heart of Jesus we find true healing. Discover how this blessed woman is healed by His Heart–and how you can be, too!

How to Use This Book

When someone goes through a difficult experience, what we see on the outside is never as revealing as what is happening inside—in that person's heart. This book is comprised of prayerful reflections that I pray will invite you to experience what the heart of the Samaritan woman and the Heart of Jesus experienced during their beautiful encounter.

Before you begin settling into this prayerful journey, let's review the structure of this book to help you better understand and reflect on this story as you read.

Prayers, Not Chapters

First, you may notice the chapters are not listed as "Chapters," but as "Prayers." Chapter 1 is listed as Prayer One (followed by a short prayer), and so on. This is to help you settle into a prayerful state before you begin reading the Bible verse at the beginning of each chapter.

The Full Story

Each chapter starts with a Scripture passage. This book will start with John 4:1 and continue through the end of the Samaritan woman story at John 4:42. Each chapter starts with a short Scripture passage from this section.

REFLECTION AND CLOSING PRAYERS

Each Scripture passage is followed by a Reflection Prayer and a Closing Prayer written using imaginative prayer, an approach of Ignatian spirituality. Both prayers are written from the heart, my heart, while I meditated and rested in the Heart of Jesus and came to understand, as one would of a dear loved one, what occurred in the depths of the heart of the Samaritan woman and the Heart of Jesus during their encounter. At first glance, both prayers might seem to be one and the same. However, there is a slight difference between the two.

The Reflection Prayer is more of a reflection of my own reaction, as well as the reflection of the heart of the Samaritan woman and the Heart of Jesus, during the events in the Bible passage. The Closing Prayer is more of a plea to God as I desire continual transformation of my own heart and seek His grace in doing so.

You may find it helpful to have your Bible handy to reference the passage in each chapter, as well as a journal to write down any thoughts or feelings you may have while reflecting on each Bible passage.

Prayer One

Jesus, take me to places unknown

Now when Jesus learned that the Pharisees had heard that Jesus was making and baptizing more disciples than John (although Jesus himself was not baptizing, just his disciples), he left Judea and returned to Galilee. He had to pass through Samaria. So he came to a town of Samaria called Sychar, near the plot of land that Jacob had given to his son Joseph.

John 4:1-5

Reflection Prayer

Jesus, Your Heart is on fire for all mankind. Each day, each moment on this earth, You strove to do Your Father's mission. On this day, this mission brought You to Sychar in Samaria. This was a place many Jews avoided, went out of their way to go around. But not You, not today. Today, the Father's will brought You to this town in need of healing, in need of renewal, in need of restoration, in need of their Savior. They desperately needed the Heart of God. And so, You came to them.

You show us in Your obedience to the Father that we, too, are always to follow Your will, even if Your will should take us out of our normal way of doing things. Your Heart burned so deeply to do the Father's will that to do anything else would have been unthinkable. You desire our hearts to burn deeply with this desire as well. You invite us into Your Heart. Jesus, immerse us in Your Heart daily, so we may be inflamed with the same desire to fulfill the Father's will You had when You walked upon this earth.

Prayer One

Closing Prayer

Jesus, immerse me in Your Heart of mercy and love. Help me to surrender to Your will so that doing anything else would be unthinkable. May I be fervent in my desire to do Your will. May I be willing to do anything and everything that You ask of me, even if it makes me uncomfortable, if it takes me to places I know not and requires sacrifice and love that know no bounds. Immerse me in Your Heart so I may never be the same again! Through Christ our Lord. Amen.

Prayer Two

Jesus, thank You for lowering Yourself to our human state

Jacob's well was there. Jesus, tired from his journey, sat down there at the well. It was about noon.

John 4:6

Reflection Prayer

Jesus, while Your Heart burned with a desire to do the Father's will, Your body was tired from the journey. You needed to sit and rest. You are fully divine, fully God, and You are also fully human in all things but sin. You consented to be like us, with a human body that required earthly nourishment and rest, because You knew the salvation You would give us by dying on the cross for us would far outweigh the limitations You would experience in Your human body. You would provide us spiritually refreshing, eternal nourishment and peace that would sustain and strengthen us even when meeting our earthly needs cannot.

What great humility, what a great gift, that the Son of God would lower Himself to the state of mortal man, that He would accept our human conditions of thirst, hunger and exhaustion. You could have reached out to the Father to relieve You from all this, but Your desire to live among us, to live like us in every way but sin, was too great.

You knew that in exposing Yourself to our plights and weaknesses, we'd be able to see that You do understand us, for You lived as we live. You were exhausted from Your journeys just as we are from ours. We know You were willing to expose Yourself to our human frailty and fatigue. From your trials, perhaps even those with the most hardened of hearts can see that our God is a God who understands our need for rest, of both body and spirit. He experienced it. He lived it. He knows what we need. At that time, the Father gave You a place to rest, this well to sit by, so You could prepare to give the spiritual respite of Your peace to the people of Samaria through the testimony of one of their own.

Closing Prayer

O God, thank You for coming to be among us, to experience life as we do. How merciful of You! You know our human frailty and our need to be understood on the most fundamental level. You came to live among us as a man, a human, like the rest of us, so that we could know Your love for us more deeply.

Give me that same spirit of humility, to lower myself and seek to understand all people, especially those who suffer and are without nourishment and rest—both in body and spirit. Help me to understand where I lack spiritual nourishment so I may throw myself into Your Heart of mercy. There, may I be enlightened with Divine wisdom and find spiritual rest. Grant me humility to see my and others' need for mercy and compassion, and the courage to spread that message and act as You desire me to act. Through Christ our Lord. Amen.

PRAYER THREE

JESUS, THANK YOU FOR ALWAYS REACHING OUT TO ME

A woman of Samaria came to draw water. Jesus said to her, "Give me a drink." His disciples had gone into the town to buy food.

John 4:7-8

Reflection Prayer

Jesus, there You sat alone as this woman came to the well. You knew her heart. You knew why she came in the heat of the day. How Your Heart was filled with understanding and compassion. You knew that relationship You were about to enter into with this woman would change the hearts of the people, her people. But first You had to start off gently, in terms she knew, in language she could understand. You desired to meet her where she was.

Oh, Jesus, how You reach out to me in prayer and times of silence with You before the tabernacle, through others, and in the world just where I am. You speak gently to my heart in words and in ways that I can understand.

Prayer Three

Closing Prayer

O God, help me to be aware of the presence of Your Spirit that is with me always. Thank You for always reaching out to me when I am in pain. Thank You for never leaving my side. Thank You for meeting me where I am, no matter the circumstances, and consoling me when I am wounded and in pain. Through Christ our Lord. Amen.

Prayer Four

Jesus, enlighten my heart with the truths of heaven

The Samaritan woman said to him, "How can you, a Jew, ask me, a Samaritan woman, for a drink?" (For Jews use nothing in common with Samaritans.) Jesus answered and said to her, "If you knew the gift of God and who is saying to you, 'Give me a drink,' you would have asked him and he would have given you living water."

John 4:9-10

Reflection Prayer

Jesus, how Your Heart must have leaped for joy as this woman did not turn her back on You. At Your request, she stopped and opened her heart and allowed You ever so slightly to enter. Curious as to Your behavior, she did not dismiss You or turn away. She asked honestly and openly about what was on her heart. She was intrigued why You, a Jew, would break with customary ways of interaction, but she was not afraid to ask the question. How Your Heart was pleased with this daughter of God, for soon she would know she was speaking with the Savior of the World, the Messiah. Soon she would know true fulfillment and joy. You continued to challenge her, to open her heart further as You led her on this journey of faith.

Prayer Four

Closing Prayer

O God, help me to allow You to enter my heart that I may receive Your love and mercy and the truths You wish to teach me. Help me not to be afraid when You reach out to me. Grant me the courage to not dismiss You when You make some request of me. Help me be open to learn more and understand what You are asking of me and how You wish to enlighten my heart by the light of Your grace. Help me to know You more as my Savior, my King, and my God. Through Christ our Lord. Amen.

PRAYER FIVE

JESUS, QUENCH MY THIRST WITH THE OCEAN OF MERCY IN YOUR HEART

[The woman] said to him, "Sir, you do not even have a bucket and the well is deep; where then can you get this living water? Are you greater than our father Jacob, who gave us this well and drank from it himself with his children and his flocks?" Jesus answered and said to her, "Everyone who drinks this water will be thirsty again; but whoever drinks the water I shall give will never thirst; the water I shall give will become in him a spring of water welling up to eternal life." The woman said to him, "Sir, give me this water, so that I may not be thirsty or have to keep coming here to draw water."

John 4:11-15

The Healing of a Wounded Heart

Reflection Prayer

Jesus, You knew the yearnings of this woman. You knew she longed to be healed. Perhaps she decided to come in the middle of the day for fear of being rejected. In this way she would be able to meet her bodily needs without having contact with those who condemned her. Your words to her must have seemed at first like a heavenly gift—to be able to avoid coming in the heat of the day for water any longer. This, on the surface, she must have ached for. But deep down, I know she thirsted for more. Your Heart must have been beating with such abundant love for her because You knew she would come to understand the meaning behind "life-giving" water. You knew she would soon no longer be afraid to venture out at any point in the day, for Your living water would fill her with courage, joy, and love—Your love. A love that would constantly renew her in each moment, each step of the way. A love that would cleanse her soul and heal her wounds so she would know who she was in God's eyes–a beautiful, pure, beloved daughter of God.

Prayer Five

Closing Prayer

Jesus, I thirst for You. I desire You. I yearn for the eternal fulfillment that only You can give. I know it is only You who can give me life-giving water. Help me to persevere in prayer. Help me to be open to what You have to speak to my heart. Help me not to run and hide, but rather to meet You at the well and be courageous in my prayer with You.

Jesus, may my thirst for Your life-giving water be deepened, a thirst always able to be quenched by Your love. When in my woundedness I seek to quench my earthly desires with the deceitful waters of the world, may I throw myself at once into the great ocean of mercy flowing forth from Your Most Sacred Heart. Through the same Christ our Lord. Amen.

PRAYER SIX

Jesus, cleanse me from my sins and restore my heart anew

Jesus said to her, "Go call your husband and come back." The woman answered and said to him, "I do not have a husband." Jesus answered her, "You are right in saying, 'I do not have a husband.' For you have had five husbands, and the one you have now is not your husband. What you have said is true."

John 4:16-18

REFLECTION PRAYER

Jesus, You knew this conversation would be difficult for this woman, so filled with pain and hurt from rejection and her own sins. So, with gentle honesty, you probed her heart and led her to acknowledge the truth. You knew she must see this and speak of it before she could move forward in faith and healing. You know this about us, too. You know we must face the truth of our sinfulness before we can move forward to a deeper faith and trust in You.

First, we must trust You with the deepest, darkest, messiest places of our hearts before we can be transformed completely into the children of God we were created to be. So, You gently called to this woman's heart to speak the truth. Surely, she could sense You received her as she was, whether she spoke up or not. Surely, she could sense Your great love for her, whether she could face the truth or not.

When we experience Your love, we also come to understand Your desire for our salvation. This understanding beckons us to leave behind our old ways of sin and embrace the truth of who we are called to be.

This understanding, this experience of Your love, is what gave her the courage to be honest with You, to acknowledge the truth of her life without fear of condemnation or rejection. This is what freed her. This is what led her to the deep healing and merciful love of Your Most Sacred Heart.

Closing Prayer

Jesus, gently call to my heart. Thank You for receiving me in all my woundedness, sin, and pain. Help me not to be ashamed to come to You as I am, not hiding, not holding anything back, ready to speak the truth of my life. Help me to know You came to save me and not condemn me. To know You came to heal and renew my heart.

Draw me closer to You in each moment, with each breath. Purify my heart and free me from the burden of my sins. I know that this healing process may be painful because my wounds are deep, and my sins have led me away from You. But I trust in You, Jesus. I know I need only turn my eyes toward You with yearning to receive You into my heart, so You may shower down Your heavenly mercy upon me and heal me. Through the same Christ our Lord. Amen.

Prayer Seven

Jesus, help me to praise You with my whole heart

The woman said to him, "Sir, I can see that you are a prophet. Our ancestors worshiped on this mountain; but you people say that the place to worship is in Jerusalem." Jesus said to her, "Believe me, woman, the hour is coming when you will worship the Father neither on this mountain nor in Jerusalem. You people worship what you do not understand; we worship what we understand, because salvation is from the Jews. But the hour is coming, and is now here, when true worshipers will worship the Father in Spirit and truth; and indeed the Father seeks such people to worship him. God is Spirit, and those who worship him must worship in Spirit and truth."

John 4:19-24

Reflection Prayer

Jesus, how Your Heart was patient with this woman as she continued to ask You the burning questions in her heart. She wanted to know. She wanted to understand. However, in her limited reasoning, she could only see how these physical places of worship were different. But You wished to give her understanding that transcended her earthly reasoning. You wished to convey to her that praise is not confined to spaces. Praising You happens in our very own hearts. It is our interior disposition that matters and what leads us to desire only that which leads to praising You.

How beautiful, how vast the places on this earth where we are able to worship You—places that lend us to turn our minds and hearts to You. Places, for example, such as the beautiful churches that direct our hearts toward the heavens and include artwork and statues that draw our attention to the saints and holy women and men of God who gave their lives totally to You. They provide a place to worship You in the flesh, in Your Eucharistic presence. There, You await us, hoping we shall come and sit with You, adore You, and praise You.

But always, and ultimately, our true praise comes from within. Our souls proclaim Your name through our actions of sacrificial love toward You and others. This is where Your

Heart was with the Samaritan woman. Soon, she would praise You before the very people who rejected her, all so she could lead them to You. Her soul reflected Your light and beckoned others to worship You and rest in Your love.

Closing Prayer

God, thank You for being patient with my questions, my curiosity, and my challenges when I do not understand. My deepest desire is to love You, but my limited reasoning gets in the way. Help me to see the vastness of heavenly possibilities that await me if only I surrender my mind and heart to You. Bestow upon me the gift of wisdom. Your desire is for us to live in Your light and to love with the same love found in Your Most Sacred Heart. Help me to remember that true praise comes from within, and to praise You for the many ways in which You bring me closer to You through people, places, and gifts in the world. Guard my heart so these people, places, and gifts do not become impediments. Allow them to only and always be signposts that lead me to Your Heart. May my heart seek to rest in You, freeing it totally for love of You alone! Through Christ our Lord. Amen.

Prayer Eight

Jesus, set my heart on fire with the truth of who You are

The woman said to him, "I know that the Messiah is coming, the one called the Anointed; when he comes, he will tell us everything." Jesus said to her, "I am he, the one who is speaking with you."

John 4:25-26

The Healing of a Wounded Heart

Reflection Prayer

Jesus, at this point, surely Your Heart must have had a burning desire to no longer hide Your true identity. The woman inched closer to the truth with each word she spoke. It was time for her to hear You say You were the Messiah. Your Heart could no longer hold back. Now was the moment You would reveal Yourself to her. You were saving this woman from her misery of sin, woundedness, and rejection, and now it was her turn to be an instrument of Your mercy to her people. Your Heart could hold back no longer. What unspeakable joy she must have felt when the heavenly revelation touched her ears. Surely the angels in heaven rejoiced when You announced Your true identity to her, for when the Son of Man speaks, all of heaven bows in adoration.

Prayer Eight

Closing Prayer

O God, help me to be brave in my relationship with You. Help me not to be afraid to bring all my questions to You. I trust that You will always lead me to the truth. May I always kneel before You in humble adoration. Thank You for this beautiful example of how to be courageous in asking You to reveal Yourself to me. Thank You for showing me how to fearlessly leave behind the world and who it says I am. Thank You for showing me how, in abandoning my heart to You, You can show me who You truly are and who I am in You, allowing You to transform my heart—a heart that You set on fire to change the world! Through Christ our Lord. Amen.

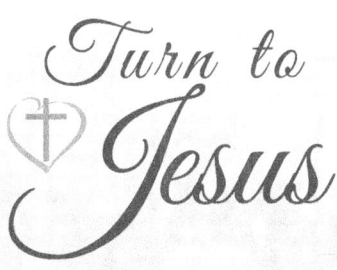

Prayer Nine

Jesus, be with me in my lack of understanding

At that moment his disciples returned, and were amazed that he was talking with a woman, but still no one said, "What are you looking for?" or "Why are you talking with her?"

John 4:27

The Healing of a Wounded Heart

Reflection Prayer

Jesus, Your disciples then returned. From their astonishment, it seems they did not understand why You would break custom. However, unlike the woman, it seems they were not comfortable asking You the questions that were on their hearts. Oh, how one day these men would become the Fathers of the Church, these men who would die to proclaim You as the Son of God. These men who would risk all to bring more hearts to Yours. They were amazed at Your words and actions. Their desire to understand and learn from You is what drew You to them and them to You. You knew what they were thinking, and soon all would be revealed.

How Your Heart loves these men and all of us who seek to understand You. How You wish for us to come to You with open hearts ready to receive Your truth, regardless of how it may affect our current understanding, knowledge, or beliefs.

Jesus, You speak to my heart, "Believe in Me. When You believe in Me, I will open My Heart to you." You wish our hearts to be open enough that we may sit down before You ready and longing to hear Your every word.

Prayer Nine

Closing Prayer

O God, help me not to be afraid to ask You all the questions in my heart. Kindle in my heart the desire to learn from You always. May my soul never cease to be amazed at Your mercy and gentle love toward me and others. When I do not understand, grant me a share in Your wisdom. Help me never to judge others or their share in what they receive from You. Help me to keep my eyes focused on You alone, grateful for the mercy You always show me. Through Christ our Lord. Amen.

Prayer Ten

Jesus, I want to love like You

The woman left her water jar and went into the town and said to the people, "Come see a man who told me everything I have done. Could he possibly be the Messiah?" They went out of the town and came to him.

John 4:28-30

REFLECTION PRAYER

At last, this woman was freed from her pain, her sins, and her woundedness! When she left her water jar behind, did she not also leave behind her shame, her guilt, and her agony? She moved in haste to share with her people—the very people who rejected her—the truth, the Good News, the news that the Messiah was among them, in their very midst, waiting for them to come to Him so He could convert their hearts, too. It seems she knew others might not listen to her if she shouted the truth, so she decided to gently lead them Your way with a question, but a question spoken boldly and without shame.

At this moment, Your Heart must have known what was occurring. You must have also known the freedom she felt, the joy, the pure desire in her heart to bring her people to You. And Your Heart desired this as well. Soon, Your newest disciple would lead them to You.

"He told me everything I have done" (John 4:39). How I imagine she said this with such freedom and without shame. She spoke from her heart that You told her everything she had done and now she was free! She stood before her people proclaiming, "Yes, He knows my sins. He knows my woundedness. He knows every part of me—every hurt, every time I've hurt others, and every time I've been rejected and betrayed. And now, I am here asking you, the very people who reject me, to come see what I've seen, to come experience what I've experienced, and to be transformed in the way He has transformed me."

In this moment had she already forgiven them? Had Your love filled her heart so deeply that she did not care how they had mistreated her? Perhaps it would still take time to completely heal; but it is clear to my heart that in this moment she only desired their good. She only desired that they encounter Your healing love. How beautiful this transformation, how glorious this miraculous healing that You bestowed on this beloved daughter of God.

Closing Prayer

Jesus, I abandon my heart to You. I desire this same kind of miraculous healing of my wounded heart. I no longer want to be ashamed, to hide from others, or to be afraid to claim who I truly am—a beloved child of God! I know I have sinned. I know I am wounded. I know I will never be worthy of Your forgiveness. I know You have already forgiven the repentant and desire me to extend forgiveness to others as well. Jesus, transform my heart and fill me with Your compassion. Jesus, help me to be so consumed in Your love that I cannot help but go out and proclaim You to the very people who have wounded me and rejected me. Jesus, I want to love like You do. Jesus, I give You my heart. I beg of You to make my heart like Yours. Through the same Christ our Lord. Amen.

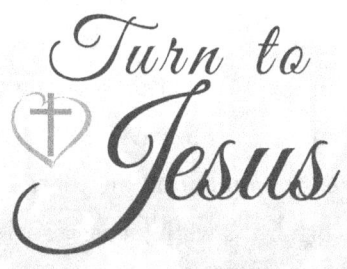

Prayer Eleven

Jesus, help me to live on the bread of life alone

Meanwhile, the disciples urged him, "Rabbi, eat." But he said to them, "I have food to eat of which you do not know." So the disciples said to one another, "Could someone have brought him something to eat?" Jesus said to them, "My food is to do the will of the one who sent me and to finish his work."

John 4:31-34

Reflection Prayer

Jesus, once again Your disciples only understood what You were saying in worldly terms. But one day they would be filled with the Spirit and would live on the bread of life. Then, these men did not understand, but Your Heart was preparing them for the day they would.

For Your food, Jesus, was to do the will of the Father. This food was Your source of strength. It lifted the burden of the sin You came to defeat, and it sustained You during Your life on earth as You pursued Your mission in this world. Your purpose was to save us from our sins. You showed us that "One does not live by bread alone, but by every word that comes forth from the mouth of God" (Matthew 4:4).

This is our call. This is where our focus should be. On the very Word of God, which is You, Jesus. We are to depend on You alone, to feed on You alone, offered to us in the Eucharist. You invite us to adore You alone in tabernacles throughout the world, to seek You and to rely on You in the most interior cell of our heart where You patiently await our response.

PRAYER ELEVEN

Closing Prayer

O God, help me to desire to live on You alone. Nourish me, sustain me, and give me the desire to live and breathe Your will and Your will alone! May this be my sole focus, my one desire. May I not deviate from Your will for my life. When I do fall from the burden of my sins, fill me with Your perseverance so I may rely on Your grace and strive to sin no more. Thank You for the times when in Your mercy, You allow me to share in the immense pain Your Heart experiences from the rejection of so many. When in my weakness I become overwhelmed with the pain You suffer, I ask that You fill me with heavenly courage so that I may rise again, renewed in Your love, and fortified in Your strength to do Your will and bring more hearts to You. Through Christ our Lord. Amen.

PRAYER TWELVE

Jesus, help me to sow the seeds of Your love

"Do you not say, 'In four months the harvest will be here'? I tell you, look up and see the fields ripe for the harvest. The reaper is already receiving his payment and gathering crops for eternal life, so that the sower and reaper can rejoice together. For here the saying is verified that 'One sows and another reaps.' I sent you to reap what you have not worked for; others have done the work, and you are sharing the fruits of their work."

John 4:35-38

Reflection Prayer

Jesus, here You gave Your disciples more insight into their baptismal role—a role we all have—as nourishing instruments of Your love in this garden of life. Some days we may sow the seed of Your love. Other days we may be a witness to another testifying to their total faith and trust in You. We are only Your instruments. We are to put ourselves into Your hands and allow You to guide us and use us as You see fit to bring others home to Your Heart.

Here, the disciples would witness the coming of a people to their acknowledgment of You as their Messiah. They would see the fruits of those who came before them who spread the message that the Messiah was coming. And now they would see the fulfillment of joy in the Samaritan people's eyes as they saw You for who You truly are–their Lord, their Savior, their God, and their King. How blessed these disciples were to be party to such a magnificent gift of heavenly mercy.

Soon these disciples would not only fulfill their baptismal role, but would assume a ministerial responsibility, acting in Your person, Christ Jesus, bringing You to us through the Eucharist. Their witness would bear fruit for generations to come. They would spread the message of Your resurrection, and this witness, this truth, is what many of them would die for.

How Your Heart was ready for Your disciples to be witnesses to this conversion. You knew this would be another stone on the path of their own journey to heaven. They would look back on this after Your resurrection and, filled with the Spirit in them, they would have a greater understanding of what occurred this day.

Renewed in their faith and trust in You, Your Heart would be their source of strength. They would be instruments of Your love and mercy. They would be bearers of the faith, just as this Samaritan woman was to her people.

Closing Prayer

O God, help me to always be willing to allow You to use me as You see fit to bring more hearts to You. Help me to be content with knowing I only need to say yes to You in each moment. Calm my thoughts so I do not worry about what the results or outcomes will be in the situations You lead me to.

When I spread the message of Your love, may I not be discouraged when others do not seem to hear the truth. Remind me that in the greatest moments in the need of others, "sowing the seed of Your truth" may mean saying nothing at all but simply looking gently upon them with Your love. Help me continue to move in faith and trust that You will lead them home to Your Heart. May I not presume to be "their Savior." Humble me with the understanding that *You* alone are the Savior of all. I am just Your lowly servant.

Help me to be content with knowing I have already found my heavenly home in Your Heart, which overflows with love for me and fulfills every one of my deepest desires as long as I keep my eyes focused on You! Through Christ our Lord. Amen.

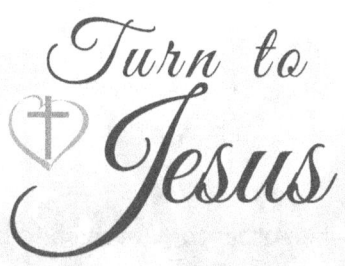

PRAYER THIRTEEN

JESUS, MAY YOU REIGN IN MY HEART FOR ALL ETERNITY

Many of the Samaritans of that town began to believe in him because of the word of the woman who testified, "He told me everything I have done." When the Samaritans came to him, they invited him to stay with them; and he stayed there two days. Many more began to believe in him because of his word, and they said to the woman, "We no longer believe because of your word; for we have heard for ourselves, and we know that this is truly the savior of the world."

John 4:39-42

Reflection Prayer

What joy must have filled the heart of this woman as she heard them express that they now believed in You because they heard for themselves. For the true joy of discipleship comes when the hearts now sit at Your feet and hear the sweet whispers of heavenly wisdom and comfort that come from Your lips. The true disciple, such as this beautiful Samaritan woman, desires to lead others to You so You can transform their hearts from the inside out, showering them with Your love and healing them with the soothing balm of Your mercy.

I wonder if, when her people came to meet You, she knew that not only did You come to transform her, but You came to transform her people, too. Undoubtedly, she must have pondered Your goodness deep within her heart. Truly forgiven herself, and as she must have sincerely forgiven them already at this point, she could rejoice purely in their conversion of heart, just as the angels rejoiced in hers.

What multitude of conversions hinged on this beautiful woman's courageous and fearless encounter with You? With humility she acknowledged her sinfulness, and then with the same humility received Your mercy. She continued in her prayerful courage and received the life-giving Spirit that freed her from her sins and woundedness. You

Prayer Thirteen

then led her into the precise place, in the exact time of day, among the very same people she could not fathom being with just hours earlier.

And how Your Heart was filled with joy as You looked upon this beautiful new disciple of Yours. What great love You have for her and what great mercy You continued to bestow on her from that day forth. It is the same joy in Your Heart that You have for us as we come to You in our sinfulness and woundedness, receive Your mercy, and become bearers of that mercy to the world.

How sweet Your victorious reign in my heart, my dear Jesus. Oh, the miracles You work in a heart when it surrenders itself into its rightful place–into Your Most Sacred Heart. The peace and healing it experiences are indescribable. And yet, it is only a glimpse of the ecstasy and pure joy we will know once we reach our heavenly homeland.

May we no longer be slaves to sin. Instead, may we be totally devoted to You! What consolation this brings to Your Heart, my dear Jesus. May we all seek to console Your Heart in every moment of every day!

Closing Prayer

Jesus, how I wish for a surrendered heart like this beautiful Samaritan woman. So brave, so humble, so inflamed with Your love and mercy! Jesus, probe my heart and flush from my eyes the sand and grit that keep me from seeing Your work in the world, and even within myself. I understand this will be painful, but I will gladly endure the purification of my soul if it means I can walk in freedom from my shame, guilt, sinfulness, and woundedness.

I no longer want to hold back from what seems like an insurmountable climb to holiness. I know the mountain is steep, but I desire nothing less than complete conformity to Your will. Jesus, I am ready. I am ready to give You everything. I am ready to confess the error of my ways and to acknowledge the truth of how I am blind when I focus on myself and not on You.

Jesus, enlighten me as You enlightened this beautiful Samaritan woman. I know You will speak gently, with firm love, with kindness, and with mercy. I unite myself to Your Heart, and I offer it as a gift to the Father for the pain You endured as You bore the pain of my sins on the cross.

Jesus, I am all Yours now. You are the Lord of my heart. Jesus, may You reign in my soul for all eternity. Through the same Christ our Lord. Amen.

About the Author

Laura Marie Durant is the prayerful servant of the Healing Heart of Jesus ministry. She writes prayers and reflections, and provides prayer support products, including prayer cards and greeting cards, which are meant for anyone who struggles with anxiety, depression, and emotional wounds, as well as for those who care for them. She started this ministry in response to a call to spread the message of the mercy, healing, and love found in the Sacred Heart of Jesus. She has received great healing through daily prayer before Jesus in the adoration chapel, experiencing what it means to rest in His Heart.

She is a Catholic Christian and has a strong love for Carmelite spirituality. Living Carmelite spirituality has transformed her prayer life and brought her to a greater love of the Immaculate Heart of Mary and the Sacred Heart of Jesus. She is humbled by the many blessings Our

The Healing of a Wounded Heart

Lord has given her and her husband to allow them to spread His love through this ministry. She prays these reflections bring anyone who reads them closer to the Sacred Heart of Jesus through the Immaculate Heart of Mary.

She is also the author of *The Passion Suffered by the Heart of Jesus: Prayerful Reflections on the Stations of the Cross*, which is a prayerful journey with Jesus that moves station-by-station through His Passion.

She lives in Central Texas with her husband, John, and attends St. Margaret Mary Catholic Church in Cedar Park, Texas. She received her bachelor's degree in psychology from the University of Texas at Austin, and a master's degree in professional counseling from Texas State University-San Marcos.

www.ingramcontent.com/pod-product-compliance
Lightning Source LLC
Chambersburg PA
CBHW071252070526
44583CB00017B/2433